I0411184

The Basics of Bartending

Bender Barware

Bender Barware

Copyright © 2016 Bender Barware

All rights reserved.

ISBN: **1539933830**
ISBN-13: **978-1539933830**

CONTENTS

CHAPTER 1

INTRODUCTION

Mixology seems to be the new buzzword when it comes to fixing drinks. It sounds like some new science taught in college these days. However, the term mixology was used way back in 1908 by "Cocktail" Bill Boothby.

The term became more popular in the 1940's when both men and women wore hats, men's suits were double breasted and the hem of a lady's dress was well below the knee. Prohibition had recently ended in America and everyone was home from WWII. Paramount released Key Largo with Bogart and Bacall and MGM came out with The Three Musketeers. Life was grand and anyone who was anyone drank Martinis, Singapore Slings, and Sidecars. Tom Collins was a popular drink along with the Manhattan and let's not forget the Old Fashioned. And advertisements even showed Schlitz Malt Liquor being served in glasses on a silver tray.

While our culture has changed immensely since the 1940's, these classic cocktails are still around and are still consumed in large quantities. We have also expanded our tastes to include flavored Vodkas and we have added cinnamon to our whiskey. In addition, we have new modern classics like the Expat, the Democrat (named for Harry Truman) and the Easy Street. In fact, the overall yearly sales of distilled spirits in the United States has reached in the billions.

With that being said, there are still only six basic liquors and the equipment used to make our libations are still pretty standard. In the next few chapters, we'll go over these base liquors. We will not, however, go into all the different beers and wines because those are different animals altogether.

We will cover the basics of bartending, the essential tools you'll need, glassware, basic terms and the recipes any bartender, whether a professional mixologist or a home bartender should know.   Let's get started!

CHAPTER 2

THE 6 BASE LIQUORS

Brandy (80 proof or40% alcohol/volume) - Brandy is distilled alcohol that has been extracted from fruit. Most brandy is made from grapes. In fact, the word brandy comes from the Dutch word for burnt wine. Other fruits used to make brandy are apricots, peaches, cherries, and blackberries.

There are two types of brandy; regular and pomace. Pomace brandy uses the skins and peels of the fruit as well as the juice. Grappa and Pisco are a couple of examples of pomace brandy.

Most brandy is aged some of the time in oak barrels and this is not only where the amber color comes from but part of the flavor as well.

There are different styles of brandy also. I'm sure you have heard of Cognac and possibly Armagnac. These styles of brandy refer to the region of France where this specific brandy is produced. Armagnac has a fruitier taste where Cognac has more of a caramel flavor to it. And in general, younger brandies have a lighter fruit taste and a more aged brandy has more of a dried fruit and spice taste to it.

France is not the only country to produce brandy, however. Italy, Portugal, Germany, South Africa and Spain also produce brandy. Even American brandy is gaining in respect and popularity.

American brandy comes from Oregon and California and is made from fermented apple cider. American brandy must be aged at least two years and be over 70 proof.

Brandy used to be served neat in a snifter. Gentlemen in smoking jackets and ascots come to mind. But today, brandy is used to make wonderful cocktails like the Brandy Alexander, Zombie, Paradise, Brandy Sour and the Jack Rose.

Gin (80 – 94 Proof or 40-47% alcohol) - Gin is a dry herbal liquor and has a piney essence to it. Gin is distilled from grains like corn, rye, wheat or barley. Gin's piney flavor comes from the Juniper berry but this spirit can also be flavored with a wide variety of botanicals.

Gin is a clear liquid that typically isn't aged so there is no age qualifier for it. And because Gin is dry, it is great for non-sweet cocktails. Gin is usually used in mixed drinks with just a few ingredients which include herbs and light fruit.

Gin was originally used as medicine back in the 17th Century. A doctor from the Netherlands developed it to help with failing kidneys.

There are 5 Kinds of Gin:

London Dry Gin (most popular) - this gin is very dry and can be infused with botanicals.

Genever - this gin is different in that it is made from malt grains which make it darker and taste more like a whiskey.

Old Tom Gin - this gin lies somewhere between the London Dry Gin and the Genever. It has a sweeter taste and was originally used in you guessed it, Tom Collins.

Plymouth Gin – this particular gin is more closely related to the London Dry Gin but it is less dry and has a subdued juniper flavor to it.

<u>New</u> <u>American</u> <u>Gin</u> - this is kind of the catch-all for all the newer gins out there. Most of these are infused with lots of other botanicals than the juniper berry.

But don't confuse these types of Gins with brands.

Some of the brands you have probably heard of are Tanqueray, Bombay Sapphire, and Beefeater. These brands are London Dry Gin.

Some mixed drinks which are made from gin are:

Martini, Gin & Tonic, Rickey, Singapore Sling, Long Island Iced Tea and the Bronx.

Rum (80 Proof/40% Alcohol) - Rum was one of the first liquors to be used in a mixed drink. Some speculate this is because of its sweet taste and versatility; although it mixes well with fruit for a tropical drink, it also provides us with many warm drinks as well.

And rum has one of the more interesting histories. The new settlers in America discovered how to make rum quite by accident in the 17th century. The production of sugar on sugarcane plantations was a real commodity for growing the economy of a fledgling nation.

When the sugar was boiled down, a thick brown substance (what we now call molasses) would ooze out of the clay pots the sugar was housed in. Initially, this substance was considered nothing more than a wasteful byproduct of sugar. Eventually, someone realized that as this goo was oozing it was also fermenting and this is when they figured out that they could distil it and make liquor out of it. Hence, we have Rum.

Nowadays there are two general types of Rum: light and dark. And once again, you guessed it, the light version is light because it has not been aged in oak casks for very long. Typically, light rum ages from 1 to 4 years. And light rum is normally produced on Caribbean Islands.

Dark Rum, on the other hand, must be aged a minimum of 3 to7 years. It not only gets its darker color from being in the oak cask longer, it also has caramel added to it. Dark rum usually comes from Haiti, Jamaica, and Martinique.

To break it down further, there are Areuerto Rican rum, Virgin Islands rum, Demeraran rum (this rum is 151 proof and used to make the drink Zombie). And there are the Haitian, Jamaican and Martinique Rums mentioned above.

Another interesting tidbit about Rum - because it's made in warmer climates, it ages about 3 times as fast as other spirits. Popular cocktails made with Rum include Daiquiri, Mojito, Hurricane, Coquito and the Bushwacker.

Whiskey (80 – 100 Proof/40 -50% Alcohol) – Whiskey or Whisky, depending on where you're from, is one of the world's if not *the* world's most popular liquor.

Whiskey is distilled from malted grains like a blend of corn, barley, rye and wheat. This liquor has a roasted oak flavor because it is usually aged in charred oak barrels. Whiskey can be straight, blended or single malt.

As a drinkable beverage, whiskey dates back to the Dark Ages and the European Christian Monasteries. It was the monks in fact that kept the distillation of this fermented grain alive during these harsh times.

Whiskey's popularity kept growing over time until the Scots perfected the process and whiskey's appeal reached the masses. Until the 18th century, that is, when the monarchy realized it could tax its citizens on their favorite drink. This is where the word "moonshine" comes into existence because secret distilleries began producing their whiskey at night using only the moon for light.

The production of whiskey continued to suffer through the American Revolution where ingredients were scarce and whiskey became currency. Apparently, nobody paid attention to what happens when you try to tax this spirit. After a while, the new government faced the angry farmers and started the now famous "Whiskey Rebellion".

Jump to the early 1800's and we have the invention of the continuous still. This contraption brought whiskey to another level. Whiskey was now a higher quality liquor and was now made available in abundance more rapidly.

It wasn't until 1920 that whiskey suffered another blow. This is when the U. S. government made it illegal to produce, transport or sell alcohol. Some say that this actually backfired because the prohibition of alcohol made it appeal to more people, especially people who lost their jobs because of prohibition and it even became acceptable for ladies to drink the "hard stuff". It took thirty years for prohibition to end and whiskey has never been more popular.

Many of the most popular drinks featuring whiskey are recipes that have been around forever. For example, Whiskey Sour, Old Fashioned, Irish Coffee and Rob Roy.

There are Bourbon whiskeys and Scotch whiskeys.

A spirit can only be called Bourbon if it follows six rules according to historian Michael Veach. First and foremost, the spirit must be produced in the U. S.. Bourbon must also contain at least 51% corn, be aged in charred white oak barrels that are new, must be distilled with less than 80% volume alcohol and put into a barrel below 62.5% alcohol volume. And last but not least, bourbon cannot contain any artificial flavors or colors.

Scotch is another whiskey. You can thank an Irish monk for giving us scotch. There are two categories of scotch; single malt and blended. A single malt scotch is made with malted barley and aged for at least three years. Blended scotch is more popular in the United States than single malt. This scotch is blended with several single malts with wheat and/or corn.

Vodka (80 – 100 Proof/40 - 50% Alcohol) -

Vodka is perhaps the most versatile of all the base liquors; it has a pretty neutral flavor. Vodka is distilled from grains like wheat, corn, rye but can also be made from potatoes.

When this spirit is distilled today, the alcohol content is high and then it is filtered through a vegetable charcoal which makes it somewhat oily. The flavor of the vodka you buy will vary greatly depending on who makes it and what flavors have been added. You can get all kinds of flavored vodka these days.

Vodka has no color to it because it typically isn't aged. And because vodka is neutral, it can be used to make drinks that are sweet and fruity or drinks that have a spicy taste.

Vodka was first produced in the 12th century using rye and was used as a medicine. And in the

14th century, Russia and Poland began producing vodka for religious ceremonies. Around the 17th century, it became customary for vodka and bread to be served at banquets before a meal.

The United States did not see vodka until the 1930's. That's because it took that long for the Smirnoff family to arrive with their very special recipe. Nowadays, vodka is the base spirit for many popular mixed drinks like the Screwdriver, Kamikaze, Bloody Mary, Sea Breeze and Vodka martinis like the Lemon Drop. And some vodkas are served straight and sipped like Cognac or Whiskey.

Tequila (80 – 100 Proof/40 – 50% Alcohol) – Tequila is unique because it is distilled from the Blue Agave plant and Tequila using 100% Agave **must** be produced in Mexico. This alcohol has an earthy tone and is semi-sweet. It can also have spicy tones as well.

There are many stories about the history of tequila and most of them are told in mythical proportions. They contain Goddesses and serpents and good vs. evil. That's why some call tequila the "Nectar of the Gods"

Because only five states in Mexico grow Agave, tequila with only Agave is very expensive. This is the tequila that you can sip like a fine whiskey or Cognac. Less expensive tequilas are blended with sugar. But to be considered tequila, the blend cannot have more than 49% sugar.

There are three kinds of tequila: Gold, Tequila Anejo, and White tequila. Gold and Tequila Anejo are aged in white oak barrels although no aging is required in the production of tequila.

The Margarita is probably the most known tequila drink in the world. There are other mixed drinks using tequila as the base that are equally good. Some are the Texas-Two-Step, Peligroso Songre, Mayan Mule and Spanish Fashion.

CHAPTER 3
BARTENDING TERMS

Now that you know about spirits in general, we'll go over bartending terms that you might come across in the future or words you have heard before but don't know what they mean.

Aperitif – A wine that is served before a meal to stimulate your appetite.

Back – A non-alcoholic drink that is served along with a shot or an especially strong drink.

Bar Spoon – A long mixing spoon. 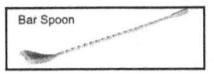 These spoons sometimes have a zester or flat surface for muddling on the other end.

Beertail – A drink where beer is the main ingredient but other distilled spirits are also added to the drink.

Behind the Stick – A phrase used for someone who goes behind the bar to give bartending a go for the first time.

Bitters – Basically the seasoning for your drink. Bitters are made with herbs and berries and have a bitter taste. Angostura is probably the most popular and well known. Bitters come in a little bottle.

Blend – To mix up the ingredients and ice in a blender.

 **Boston Shaker -** A type of shaker that consists of a mixing glass and a metal tumbler. You put the ingredients of your drink in the glass with ice and then put the tumbler, which is a little larger, on top of the glass. The ice will form a seal and you shake until the drink is very cold. You then use a Hawthorne strainer or a julep strainer to strain the drink into a glass.

Breaking the Shaker – A method of straining with a Boston shaker. You break the seal of the two tumblers and pour the drink from the crack you have made between the two halves.

Build – To make a drink. You begin with the ice and "build" by adding the alcohol, juice and then garnish.

Call Drink – When you ask for a drink to be made with a specific brand of liquor and a specific brand of mixer.

Chill – When you add ice and/or water to a glass while you mix the drink in a shaker and then remove the ice and/or water from the glass before pouring the drink into it. You can also chill a glass in the freezer without any ice.

Chaser – A mixer you drink right after a straight shot to introduce a different taste.

Cocktail – A mixture of alcohol and liqueur combined with a mixer which is often shaken.

Cooler – A bottled drink made with a variety of alcohols and different flavors.

Collins – A sour served in a tall glass with ice and soda water (Tom Collins).

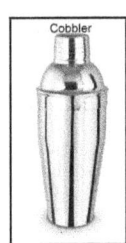

Cobbler/Standard Cocktail Shaker - This shaker is probably the most common shaker for cocktails. It consists of 2 metal tumblers with a built-in strainer.

Croptail – Mixed drinks that are made with unusual, fresh vegetables and herbs.

Dash – 1/16 ounce or less. A few drops of an ingredient.

Dirty - When you add a little olive brine to your martini.

Dry - When a dry vermouth is added to a drink.

27

Flame – Setting a drink on fire.

Float – When one alcohol sits on top of another.

Free Pouring – When you make a mixed drink without any measuring devices.

Frosted - When you put a glass or mug in the freezer it forms a frost when you take it out. Frosted glasses are great for gin and vodka drinks.

Garnish – Little pieces of fruits or herbs added to a mixed drink to enhance the flavor.

Gomme – Another name for simple syrup.

Hawthorne Strainer – Used with a Boston
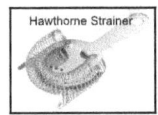
Shaker, this disc has prongs and a metal
spring. The spring fits inside the glass
and strains the liquid.

Highball – What you call a drink that contains any
spirit and then something carbonated, like a gin
and tonic.

Infusion – When you put an extra flavor like
vanilla or a fruit in a spirit and let it sit for weeks
or months to change the flavor. Today you can
purchase spirits already enhanced like flavored
vodkas.

Jigger - Usually 2-sided, this is a little
measuring cup to measure the amount of
liquor you put into a drink.

Layered – Usually served in a shot glass or a shooter, this drink contains different unmixed liquors with the heavy liquors on the bottom.

Liqueur – A neutral spirit (like vodka) which has been distilled with fruit or herbs. Liqueurs are not only served over ice, they also make a great ingredient in other mixed drinks.

Mist – An alcohol poured over crushed ice. Crushed ice chills quicker than ice cubes.

Mixers – the soft part of a mixed drink made with hard liquor. Any type of soda, tonic, or juice will do.

Mocktail – Mixed drinks that contain no alcohol.

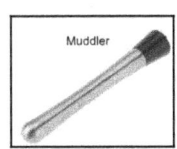 **Muddler** – the instrument used to crush herbs and fruit in the bottom of your shaker. It is made of either wood or stainless steel and looks like a miniature baseball bat.

Naked – When you make a mixed drink without stirring or shaking. You simply spray the glass with vermouth and then add your spirit straight from the bottle which is kept in the freezer into the glass. You do not use any mixer or any ice.

Neat – When you serve a drink neat, you pour the liquor into a glass (usually a shot glass) with no ice or mixer.

On the Rocks – A drink served over ice cubes. It can also be prepared up and then strained over the ice.

Perfect – A Manhattan that is not sweet or sour.

Pony – One ounce.

Poptail – Frozen ice pops that contain a distilled spirit in them.

Premium Call – A more expensive brand of liquor the customer requests.

Proof – Tells you how strong a spirit is. It is equal to ½ percent of alcohol volume. For example, if you buy 80 proof, you will get 40% alcohol volume.

Rim – This refers to rubbing a citrus peel around the rim of the glass before dropping the peel into the glass or adding salt or sugar to the rim of a glass.

Rocks – Refers to the ice your drink is poured over.

Rolling – When you gently pour your drink from one glass to another to mix the ingredients. This method is usually employed when making drinks with tomato juice in them.

Served Long – A mixed drink that is served in a Collins glass (tall glass) because it has more mixer than other mixed drinks.

Shaken – When using a cocktail shaker to mix a drink. The shake should last until the tumbler is very cold.

Shooter – Various liquors served in a shooter glass without ice. These can be layered, stirred or shaken.

Shot Glass – a little glass with a heavy bottom used when drinking a spirit in one gulp. Think tequila.

Sour – Lemon juice and sugar mixed together to be combined with a spirit like a Whiskey Sour.

 **Speed Pourer** – A tool which is attached to the lip of a bottle to facilitate the flow of liquid and helps control the amount of liquid being poured.

Speed Rail – A long stainless steel shelf or box that is attached to the bar where the most commonly used liquors sit for easier access.

Spirit - Any alcoholic beverage that has been

distilled.

Splash – A little more than a dash but less than an ounce of any liquid.

Stirred – If it is not shaken it is stirred. Stirring uses a bar spoon and is usually used when you are combining a spirit and one other ingredient.

Straight-Up – When your drink is shaken or stirred with ice and then strained into a glass without ice.

Toddy – A combination of liquor, hot water, and a sweetener served with spices in a tall glass.

Topless – When you do not put salt or sugar around the rim of a glass in recipes that usually call for it.

Twist – A piece of citrus peel used as a garnish.

Vermouth – Part of the aperitif family but stronger and infused with flavorings like herbs, bark, and roots.

Virgin – A drink that is normally made with alcohol but in this case without the liquor.

Well Drink – A drink where the brand of liquor or the mixer is not named when ordering.

Wheel – A spiral of citrus peel that is hooked onto the glass of a mixed drink. It can also be a thin slice of fruit that sits on the glass rim as a garnish.

Zest – When you grate a piece of citrus without cutting any pith. Most use a zester to do this. This adds, not only flavor but aroma.

CHAPTER 4

BARTENDING BASICS

If you are just starting to put together your first home bar, don't worry about spending wads of cash on one of everything; just start out by purchasing the alcohol you enjoy, ingredients for the drinks you like and the tools that are necessary to make your favorite cocktails.

As time goes by, you'll naturally expand on what you have and pretty soon you'll have a well-stocked bar for almost any drink for any occasion.

With that being said, below is a list of what a **complete home bar** would consist of:

- 1 bottle each of the 6 base spirits (brandy, rum, vodka, tequila, whiskey, and gin)
- 1 bottle of domestic red wine
- 1 bottle of domestic white wine
- 12 pack quality beer
- Several liqueurs like amaretto, flavored schnapps, crème de menthe or a coffee liqueur
- Ice (one of the most important parts of a cocktail!)

Other items you will need are:

- Coca-Cola (soda/diet soda)
- Sprite (lemon/lime soda)
- Ginger ale
- Club soda
- Tonic water
- Lemon and lime juice (always fresh)
- Orange and pineapple juice
- Tomato juice

(When getting ready for a party, a good rule to follow is to allow 1 bottle of whatever for 5 guests.)

The little extras needed for your bar include:

- Lemon/lime wedges
- Orange slices
- Olives
- Tobacco sauce
- Worcestershire sauce
- Bitters

Tools for the home bar include:

- Shaker (Boston or Cobbler)
- Hawthorne strainer if using a Boston shaker
- Jigger
- Bar spoon
- Muddler

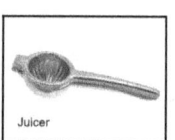

Juicer

- Speed pourers (optional)
- Hand held Juicer
- Blender
- Ice bucket
- Knife
- Small cutting board

- Swizzle sticks (if you are determined to have everything)

Now that you know a little about liquor in general, have a grasp of cocktail lingo and a list of everything you need to make a drink, let's go over the basic how-tos of bartending.

There are 5 basic rules to follow when making cocktails or mixed drinks.

1. Make sure your liquor cabinet contains good quality liquor. You don't have to buy top shelf brands but don't buy at the bottom either.

2. Use only fresh ingredients. Don't use store-bought mixers if you can help it; mixed drinks are always better with handmade mixers and simple syrups.

3. Always measure what you put into the glass. Unless you are a well- seasoned bartender, don't try to free pour anything.

Measuring equals consistency in good drinks.

4. If a recipe calls for a garnish, garnish the drink. Garnishes not only look nice they also provide a purpose. These added touches also provide aroma and taste to your cocktail.

5. Know when to chill your glass. If you keep a certain liquor in your freezer, put your glass in the freezer for a few minutes. And if you're using a shaker to mix a drink, put ice in the glass before you start shaking. This keeps the drink colder for a longer period of time.

Shaken or Stirred?

First, you probably want to follow the recipe. Another good way to decide whether you shake your drink or stir your drink is to look at the ingredients. Most of the time you are going to **shake** when the ingredients include fruit juices, simple syrup, sour mix, dairy, eggs or any cream liqueur.

You get a balanced cocktail when you shake because it not only combines the ingredients well, it also provides a little bit of melted ice which helps with the overall flavor of the drink.

Which brings us to the ins and outs of using a cocktail shaker. Sounds silly really, how hard can it be to shake? However, there are a few steps you need to follow. First, fill your shaker (if you are using a cobbler or standard shaker) half way with ice. This way, the cup starts getting cold and your other ingredients get cool when they hit the ice. Make sure you don't overfill the shaker because the drink needs room to move inside the shaker.

Put the top that covers the strainer on the shaker and while holding both the top and the bottom tumblers with one hand, shake over your shoulder enthusiastically while counting to 10 (one one thousand, two one thousand...). By the time you get to 10, the cocktail shaker should have a little bit of frost on the outside and you know your drink is ready to be strained into a glass.

You use a strainer for a couple of reasons. The shaker will have some partially melted ice in it and you don't want to pour that into the glass you are serving the drink in. Also, you may have pieces of herbs or fruit that does not belong in the finished drink like mint leaves for instance.

As mentioned earlier, the Cobbler has a built-in strainer but the Boston Shaker does not. Instead, you will need to purchase a separate strainer called a Hawthorne strainer.

With a cobbler, after you take the top off you will hold the top of the shaker where the strainer is with a couple of fingers to ensure the strainer does not come off when pouring. Hold the shaker upside down over the glass and slowly pour out the drink and shake it a tad to make sure all the liquid comes out.

With a Boston shaker, you will fit the Hawthorne strainer inside the tumbler. The strainer has a flat top with some perforations and a flexible spring on the bottom. The spring will catch any ice or solid ingredients so when you put the strainer on top of the tumbler, make sure the spring in on the bottom. Also, when you finish pouring the drink into the glass, tip the shaker back up quickly to avoid any spills.

You'll want to **stir your drink** if it does not contain any of the extra mixers. When stirring, the purpose is to combine the limited ingredients gently and let the ice melt a little bit like you do when you shake a drink to balance everything out.

Start by filling the shaker half full with ice (just like when you shake) and then add your ingredients.

When you stir, use a bar spoon because it is longer and should have a twisted stem to help with the stirring. Also, make sure you stir slowly and steadily.

There are different ways bartenders use a bar spoon; some hold the spoon between their thumb and the next two fingers at the top of the spoon where the twist begins and twirls the spoon for about 20 seconds while also moving the spoon up and down. And some rotate the spoon evenly around the shaker for about 20 seconds.

If your drink requires **muddling**, there's a technique for that too. And this technique requires a muddler. If you read over the bartending lingo above, you know that a muddler is a tool used to crush fruit and/or herbs and spices together at the bottom of a shaker for certain cocktails.

The object when using a muddler is not to make a mush at the bottom of the shaker or glass. Instead, you are trying to release the oils and juices of the ingredients you are muddling. Make sure to do the muddling before you add anything else to the shaker or glass. You will gently press down on the ingredients and give it a half turn. You will do this several times.

If you are a fan of fruity frozen drinks, here's how to **blend** these cocktails perfectly.

You want to start by blending the fruit, liquor and juices before you add any ice. As a side note, if your blender's top comes in two pieces and the center is removable, this makes a great measuring device. Also, if you cube your own fruit, make them about an inch square.

Back to blending. After blending everything, add your ice. Start by adding about a cup of ice for every serving and add more ice as you go along. If it all possible, use cracked ice or small ice cubes so your blender will not have to work too hard.

Start the blender at a slower speed and work your way up the buttons to a faster speed. This helps avoid having any chunks in the pitcher when you have finished blending.

When your blender sounds like there is no more ice chopping, stop the blender and check what's inside. If your pitcher is too watery, add more ice and continue blending. If it is too chunky, add more liquid to it. Preferably one of the ingredients already in the drink.

CHAPTER 5

GLASSWARE

If you are just beginning to build up your bar, chances are you have glassware already; in your kitchen. If money is tight, use what you have. Even mason jars are popular drinking glasses these days!

When you do purchase your first set of glassware, think about what drinks you enjoy making and drinking. Glasses you use for the bar are shaped differently for a reason. These different shapes contribute to the flavor of the drinks you are serving.

There's a rule of thumb that states: if you are serving a drink that is *shaken* or *stirred* and the drink is served *with no ice*, use a glass with a stem. This would be what most people call a martini glass but is actually a cocktail glass. You want to use the stem to hold the glass so that your hands don't warm the drink. Another type of glass for these drinks is the coupe.

If you are building the drink in the glass (usually over ice), you will use an old fashioned or rocks glass. This glass can also be called a tumbler. The old fashion glass holds 6-8 ounces but you can also get a double old fashioned which holds 12-14 ounces.

For drinks that call for fruit juice or other liquids and lots of ice use a Collins glass or highball glass. Most of these drinks require more juice than what an old fashioned will hold to make the drink taste good.

The highball glass holds 8-12 ounces while the Collins glass holds 12-16 ounces.

This rule, however, doesn't cover all glassware. Some mixed drinks are served in their own glasses and beer and wine are served in a multitude of different glasses depending on the kind beer or wine you are serving.

To make it easier, listed below are pictures of most glassware along with descriptions of what goes in them. We'll start with mixed drinks and cocktail glasses and move on to beer and then wine glasses.

- **Cocktail Glass** – (usually holds 8 ounces) This glass has a triangular shaped bowl. The shape of the cocktail glass helps the ingredients from separating and the stem keeps the drink cold when holding. But don't fill it completely to the top because it will spill easily. Some drinks served in this glass include martinis and manhattans.

- **Coupe** – (holds about 8 ounces) This glass is what we drank champagne in 40 years ago. Nowadays it holds cocktails like daiquiris, manhattans and sidecars.

- **Coupette / Margarita** – (6-10 ounces) Used for serving frozen drinks or margaritas.

-  **Hurricane** – This glass is shaped like a hurricane globe and holds drinks like the Long Island Iced Tea and the Zombie as well.

- **Liqueur / Cordial** – (1-3 ounces) Use this glass if you are serving any type of liqueur or layered shots.

- **Brandy Snifter / Cognac / Balloon** – (8-14 ounces) This glass is short stemmed with a wide bottom and a fairly narrow top. The wide bottom is for swirling the liquid to release the aromas which then get caught at the top. Also, the rounded bottom allows your hands to cup the bowl for warming.

- **Old Fashioned / Rocks Glass** (6-8 ounces) Use this glass if you are building the drink in the glass over ice.

- **Highball** - (8- 12 ounces) This glass looks like

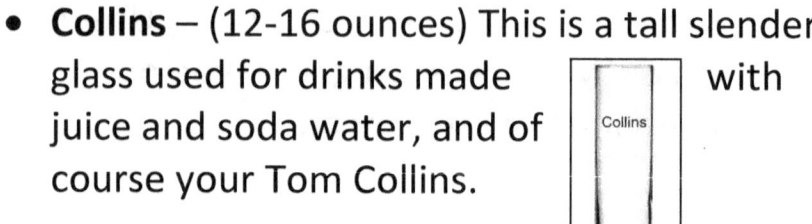

your average glass in the kitchen cabinet. If you make a drink with juice this is a good glass to use.

- **Collins** – (12-16 ounces) This is a tall slender glass used for drinks made with juice and soda water, and of course your Tom Collins.

- **Shot Glass / Shooter / Whiskey** – (1.25-1.5 ounces) These glasses are bottom heavy and are used to measure liquor or serve liquor in which is gulped in one shot.

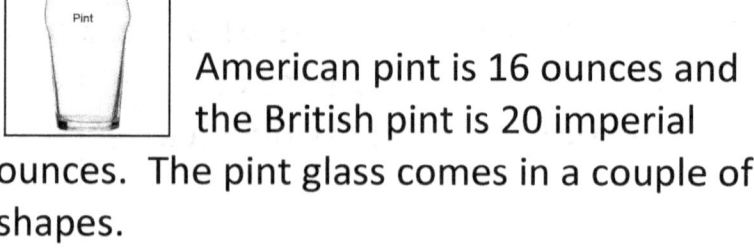

- **Pint Glass** – (16 ounces) The pint glass is probably the most popular glass for serving beer. The

American pint is 16 ounces and the British pint is 20 imperial ounces. The pint glass comes in a couple of shapes.

Conical – As the name suggests, this glass is shaped like a cone with the wider part at the top. The shape allows for easy stacking and the wider top allows for the aroma to escape.

Nonic – This pint glass has a wider lip close to the top of the glass. This glass is designed for better holding.

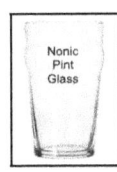

- **Pilsner** – This beer glass is tall, slender and tapered, and usually holds 12 ounces. The shape helps to hold a good head.

- **Stange** – A traditional German beer glass, the word means "stick" which denotes the tall slender shape of this beer glass. It is used to serve more delicate beers to showcase the malt and hops in these beers.

- **Weizen** – This is a Bavarian glass used for serving wheat beer. The walls are thin which helps hold the head.

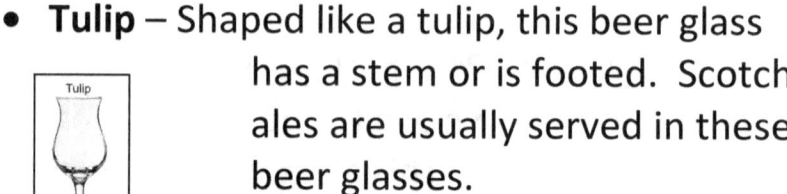

- **Tulip** – Shaped like a tulip, this beer glass has a stem or is footed. Scotch ales are usually served in these beer glasses.

- **Snifter** – This same glass used to serve brandy and Cognac, also serves as a beer glass for strong ales because the liquid can be swirled and the aromas unleashed.

- **Goblet / Chalice** – This glass is a bowl with a round-footed stem. The glass is thicker with a goblet than a chalice. Most drink Belgian ales in this type of glass.

Beer Mug – This type of beer glass comes in all sizes and has a handle. The glass is very thick which helps to insulate the beer to keep it cool. Some beer mugs have dimples on them so the drinker can enjoy the  overall color and clarity of what they are consuming.

- **Beer Stein** – Beer steins are very similar to beer mugs but steins have a hinged lid with a lever for your thumb to push open. Also, steins can be made from different materials like wood, stone, porcelain or pewter. Most beer steins today are bought for their ornamental features and are not used for drinking.

- **Tasting & Sampler Glass** – These beer glasses typically hold 2 ½ to 6 ounces and are used mostly by brewery tours. They come in all sizes and shapes however and are

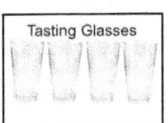

becoming quite popular with craft beer enthusiasts.

Before we cover the different types of wine glasses, let's preface this by saying there are two schools of thought on wine glasses. Some wine enthusiasts believe that it does not matter what kind of glass you use for wine because it is the wine and not the glass that is important. They believe that different wine glasses for different wines is nothing more than great marketing. Others, however, stick to the thought that wines glasses are made differently depending on the type of wine made and a special shape of glass to enhance the taste, aroma and experience of drinking wine.

- **All-Purpose Wine Glass** – If you are just starting out or are low on funds, this is a great wine glass for you. This wine glass is in between a red wine glass and a white wine glass.

- **Red Wine Glass** – This is a large wine glass with a large bowl so more of the wine is exposed to the air. You want this exposure because the aromas and flavors are complex than other wines. The bowl is wide so that you can place your nose close to the wine for smelling.

Bordeaux Wine Glass – This glass is taller than the average red wine glass but with a slightly smaller bowl. This glass is recommended for full 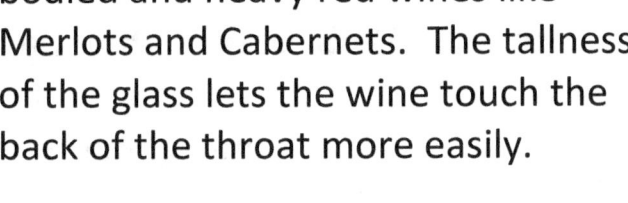 bodied and heavy red wines like Merlots and Cabernets. The tallness of the glass lets the wine touch the back of the throat more easily.

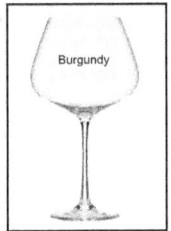 **Burgundy Wine Glass** – The burgundy glass is for a full bodied but a lighter red wine. The glass is not as tall as the Bordeaux glass but the bowl is bigger so that the wine will hit the tip of the tongue first to taste the delicate flavors. You should

serve a Pinot Noir in this type of wine glass.

- **White Wine Glass** – For white wines, the bowl of these glasses are more of a U shape and a little more upright than bowls of red wine glasses. Because white wine is served chilled, this bowl shape not only helps to keep the wine cold longer, it also helps to release the aromas of the wine.

- **Sparkling Wine Glass / Champagne Flute** – Used for sparkling wines and champagne, these glasses are very narrow to allow the carbonation to remain longer, giving it the bubbles which are made during fermentation.

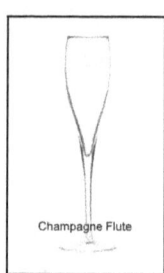

- **Rose´ Wine Glass** - There are two different shapes that a rose wine glass comes in.  One is a footed glass with a short bowl that tapers slightly. Or you can use a glass that flairs a little on top. If you don't have either of these glasses, use a white wine glass.

- **Port / Dessert Wine Glass** – Dessert wines and fortified wines usually contain more alcohol in them than other wines. For this reason, you need a small wine glass for these wines. You would use the same kind of glass used for serving sherry or a cordial.

- **Stemless Wine Glass** – These wine glasses are very popular today. One reason may be because they are easier to handle and don't break as easily. In any case, you can find stemless wine glasses with different bowl shapes depending on the type of wine you serve.

CHAPTER 6
COCKTAIL RECIPIES

Now that we have covered the basics of bartending, let's get down to the drink recipes. We'll start with five iconic recipes because these are the recipes that every bartender should know.

Martini

Ingredients

- Ice
- 4 ounces gin
- 1 ounce dry vermouth (sometimes called French or white vermouth)
- Lemon peel
- Olive

Directions

Pour gin and vermouth into a mixing glass over ice and stir well. Strain into a chilled cocktail glass.
Squeeze lemon peel over drink and discard.
Garnish with 1 green olive.

This recipe is for the classic martini. There are different variations of this drink.   If someone asks you for:

Dry Martini or **Extra Dry** - use less vermouth

In and Out - pour vermouth over ice into the mixing glass and stir for a second then pour everything out before adding the gin

Perfect - use equal parts sweet and dry vermouth

Sweet - use all sweet vermouth and garnish with a cherry instead of an olive

Tom Collins

Ingredients

- Ice
- 1 ½ ounces gin
- ½ ounce simple syrup
- Juice of ½ lemon (about 1 ½ tablespoons)
- Soda water
- Orange slice
- Maraschino cherry

Directions

Fill your shaker with ice and then add the gin, lemon juice, and the simple syrup. Shake hard for about 30 seconds. When the shaker gets very cold you're done. Strain into a glass filled with ice and top it off with an orange slice and a maraschino cherry.

Manhattan

Ingredients

- Ice
- 3 ounces Canadian or Rye whiskey
- 1 ounce sweet vermouth (red)
- 1 dash bitters (Angostura or Peychaud's)

Directions

Fill shaker or mixing glass with ice and pour in all ingredients. Stir until the drink is very cold, letting the ice melt down the drink some. Pour into a cocktail glass and garnish with a maraschino cherry.

Old Fashioned

Ingredients

- Ice
- 2 ounces bourbon or rye whiskey
- ½ ounce simple syrup

- 2 dashes angostura bitters
- Orange twist
- Maraschino cherry

Directions

Fill shaker with ice and add whiskey, syrup and bitters. After a good shake, strain the drink into a glass with ice and then garnish with an orange twist.

Bloody Mary

Ingredients

- Ice
- 1 ¼ ounces vodka
- 2 ½ ounces tomato juice
- Dash of Worcestershire Sauce
- Dash of Tobasco Sauce
- Dash of salt and pepper
- Celery stalk

Directions

Fill a tall glass with ice and pour in the vodka. Add the Worcestershire Sauce, Tobasco Sauce and salt and Pepper. Stir with a cocktail spoon and garnish with a celery stick.

Other Great Cocktail Recipes

Apple Martini

Ingredients

- Ice cubes
- 2 ounces vodka
- 1 ½ ounces sour apple liqueur
- 1 ½ teaspoons fresh lemon juice
- Granny Smith apple slice

Directions

Fill shaker between ½ and ¾ full with ice. Add vodka, sour apple liqueur, and lemon juice.

Cover and shake while counting to ten. You know it is ready when there is condensation or frost on the outside of the shaker.

Strain martini into a chilled cocktail glass and garnish with the apple slice.

Autumn Apple

Ingredients

- Ice cubes
- 2 ounces dry gin
- 3 teaspoons fresh lemon juice
- 3 teaspoons honey syrup (mix honey and sugar on stovetop until sugar melts. Store in refrigerator.)
- 1 pinch cinnamon
- 1 dash bitters
- Lemon twist

Directions

Fill shaker half way with ice. Add gin, lemon juice, honey syrup, cinnamon, and bitters.

Shake for 10 seconds and strain drink into a cocktail or coupe glass that has been chilled.

Aviation

Ingredients

- Ice cubes
- 1 ½ ounces gin
- 3 teaspoons fresh lemon juice
- ¾ ounce maraschino liqueur
- 2 maraschino cherries

Directions

Fill shaker about half way with ice. Add gin, lemon juice, and maraschino liqueur. Put top on the shaker and shake until condensation or frost appears on the shaker.

Strain drink into a cocktail or coupe glass and top with cherries.

Bloody Bulldog

Ingredients

- Ice cubes
- 4 ounces tomato juice
- 2 ounces gin (gets its name from Bulldog gin)
- 3 teaspoons fresh lemon juice
- ½ clove of garlic (1/4 teaspoon minced garlic)
- 1 tablespoon horseradish
- 1 tablespoon balsamic vinegar
- 1 tablespoon Worcestershire sauce
- 3 dashes celery salt
- Tobasco sauce
- Celery stick

Directions

This drink is stirred rather than shaken.

Fill a cocktail shaker with ice until half full. Add all ingredients are combined thoroughly.
Strain drink into a highball glass filled with ice.
Add celery stick.

Bourbon Sweet Tea by the Glass

Ingredients

- Ice cubes
- 1 cup sweetened iced tea
- 1 ounce bourbon
- 1 lemon wedge
- Mint leaves

Directions

Fill your highball glass with ice and add sweet tea and bourbon. Stir gently.   Squeeze lemon wedge into drink and add the wedge to the glass. Put a mint leaf on top.

Bourbon Sweet Tea by the Pitcher

Ingredients

- 4 cups boiling water
- 1 cup sugar
- 12 tea bags (black tea if you have it)
- 6 cups cold water

- 4 cups crushed ice
- 1 bottle bourbon (750 ml)

Directions

Put sugar in a hot proof pitcher. Boil 4 cups of water and when water starts boiling, add the tea bags and turn the stove off.

After about 10 minutes, remove the tea bags and pour into the pitcher. Stir until all sugar is dissolved. Add the bottle of bourbon, 6 cups cold water along with 4 cups of ice. Keep stirring until the liquid is no long hot.

Cover and put into the refrigerator for about 2-3 hours. When cold, fill a highball glass with ice and pour your tea. You can garnish with a mint leaf and/or lemon wedge.

Brandy Sour

Ingredients

- Ice cubes
- 2 ounces brandy
- 3 teaspoons lemon juice
- 1 teaspoon superfine sugar
- Orange slice
- Cherry

Directions

Fill cocktail shaker half full with ice. Add the brandy, lemon juice, and sugar. Put the top on and shake for 10 seconds.

Strain drink into a chilled cocktail glass and garnish with an orange slice and a cherry.

Bronx

Ingredients

- Ice cubes
- 1 ½ ounces dry gin
- ¾ ounce dry vermouth
- ¾ ounce sweet vermouth
- 1 ounce fresh orange juice
- Orange twist

Directions

Fill shaker half way with ice. Add gin, both types of vermouth and orange juice. Shake for 10 seconds.

Strain drink into a chilled cocktail glass and garnish with an orange twist.

Bushwacker

Ingredients

- Ice cubes
- ounce rum
- ½ ounce vodka
- ½ ounce Baily's Irish Cream liqueur
- ½ ounce Kahhlua
- ½ ounce amaretto liqueur
- ½ ounce chocolate-flavored liqueur
- ½ ounce Frangelico or any hazelnut liqueur
- ½ ounce crème de coconut
- 1 cup crushed ice
- 3 dashes of grated nutmeg
- 1 tablespoon whipped cream
- Maraschino cherry

Directions

Put all the liquid ingredients in a blender. Combine these ingredients well. Add Ice and keep blending until you have the consistency of a milkshake.

Pour finished drink into tulip glasses, add whipped cream and sprinkle with nutmeg. Top them off with a cherry.

Californication

Ingredients

- Ice cubes
- ¾ ounce vodka
- ¾ ounce gin
- ¾ ounce rum
- ¾ ounce tequila
- ½ ounce orange liqueur
- 3 teaspoons lemon juice
- 4 ½ tablespoons orange juice

Directions

Fill shaker half way with ice. Add all ingredients and gently stir. Strain into a highball glass filled with ice.

Cherry Collins

Ingredients

- Ice cubes
- 2 ounces vodka
- ¾ ounce fresh lemon juice
- ¾ ounce simple syrup
- Club soda
- Bing cherry

Directions

Fill a highball glass with ice. Add vodka, lemon juice, and simple syrup. Stir gently and then add club soda. Top off with a Bing cherry or two. You build this drink in the glass because it contains club soda.

Cosmopolitan

Ingredients

- Ice cubes
- 1 cup vodka
- ½ cup triple sec
- ½ cup cranberry juice
- ¼ cup fresh lime juice

Directions

Fill cocktail shaker half full with ice cubes. Add all ingredients and shake for 10 seconds. Strain drink into a chilled cocktail glass.

Coquito (Puerto Rican Eggnog)

Ingredients

- Ice cubes
- 2 cans coconut cream
- 1 can sweetened condensed milk
- 1 small can evaporated milk
- 1 teaspoon vanilla extract

- 1 ½ cups rum
- 1 tablespoon ground cinnamon
- 1 tablespoon ground nutmeg

Directions

Put liquid ingredients in a blender (not the ice…yet).
Blend until combined well. Add ice and blend on high for about 5 minutes.

Pour the coquito into a pitcher, cover and refrigerate for about 30 minutes.

Serve in Irish coffee mugs or tulip glasses.

Crownberry Apple

Ingredients

- Ice cubes
- 1 ½ ounces apple flavored whiskey (Crown Royal has a great apple whiskey)
- 4 ounces cranberry juice

Directions

Fill rocks or old fashioned glass with ice. Add whiskey and cranberry juice. Stir gently.

Daquiri

Ingredients

- Ice cubes
- 1 ½ ounces light rum
- 2 tablespoons fresh lime juice
- 1 teaspoon simple syrup

Directions

Fill shaker half way with ice cubes. Add rum, lime juice and syrup. Shake for 10 seconds. Pour into a chilled cocktail glass.

Democrat

Ingredients

- Ice cubes

- 2 ounces vodka
- 2 ounces ginger liqueur
- 2 tablespoons fresh lime juice
- Splash simple syrup
- 2 dashes orange bitters
- Club soda
- Thin orange slice
- Slice of lime

Directions

Fill a rocks or old fashioned glass with ice. Build this drink in the order of ingredients listed. Stir with a bar spoon **before** you add the club soda. Top off with club soda and add lime slice to glass.

Easy Street

Ingredients

- Ice cubes
- 1 ½ ounces gin
- 1 ½ tablespoons fresh lemon juice
- 1 ½ tablespoons elderflower liqueur
- 1 ½ teaspoons simple syrup
- 3 thin cucumber slices

- 2 ounces club soda

Directions

Put gin, lemon juice, liqueur, simple syrup and 2 of the cucumber slices into a cocktail shaker. Muddle what you have so far. Add about 1 ½ cups ice to shaker and shake vigorously for 10 seconds.

Strain into a Collins glass filled with ice. Top off with club soda and add cucumber slice to drink for garnish.

El diablo

Ingredients

- Ice cubes
- 1 ½ ounces tequila
- 3 teaspoons crème de cassis (dark red liqueur made from black currants)
- 3 teaspoons lime juice
- Ginger beer

- Lime wedges

Directions

Add tequila, crème de cassis and lime juice to a half filled cocktail shaker. Shake hard for 10 seconds.

Fill an old fashioned or rocks glass with ice and strain cocktail over ice. Top drink off with ginger beer and add a lime wedge or two for garnish.

Expat

Ingredients

- Ice cubes
- 2 ounces bourbon
- 2 tablespoons fresh lime juice
- 1 ½ tablespoons simple syrup
- Mint leaf
- Dash of Angostura bitters

Directions

Fill a cocktail shaker with ice until half full. Add all ingredients except for the mint leaf and dash of bitters. Shake well for at least 10 seconds.

Strain into a chilled coupe or cocktail glass and garnish with mint leaf and bitters.

Gimlet

Ingredients

- Ice cubes
- 2 ounces gin
- 1 ½ tablespoons fresh lime juice
- 1 ½ tablespoons simple syrup
- Fresh lime wheel

Directions

Fill a cocktail shaker with ice half way. Add gin, lime juice, and simple syrup. Using a bar spoon, stir until the drink is very cold.

Strain gimlet into a rocks glass with ice or a chilled cocktail glass with no ice. Garnish with a lime wheel.

Gin and Tonic

Ingredients

- Ice cubes
- 2 ounces gin
- 4 ounces tonic water
- 1 tablespoons fresh lime juice
- Lime wedge

Directions

Fill Collins glass with ice. Pour in gin, tonic water, and lime juice. Gently stir with a bar spoon until combined. Add a lime wedge for garnish.

Hurricane

Ingredients

- Ice cubes
- 2 ounces light rum
- 2 ounces dark rum
- 2 ounces passion fruit syrup
- 1 ounce fresh orange juice
- 1 ounce fresh lime juice
- Thick slice of orange cut in half

Directions

Fill cocktail shaker half full with ice. Add all ingredients and shake vigorously for 10 seconds.

Strain into a hurricane glass filled with ice. Place orange slice on the rim of glass.

Irish Coffee

Ingredients

- 1 cup coffee, freshly brewed and hot

- 1 tablespoon brown sugar
- 1 ½ ounces Irish whiskey
- Whipped heavy cream

Directions

Preheat a glass footed coffee mug. You put it in the microwave if microwave proof or pour very hot water into a glass and then pour out.

Fill a hot mug about ¾ full of hot coffee. Add brown sugar and stir until sugar is dissolved. Add Irish whiskey and blend with a bar spoon. Top coffee off with a dollop of whipped cream.

Jack Rose

Ingredients

- Ice cubes
- 2 ounces Applejack (brandy distilled from apples)
- 1 ounce fresh lemon juice
- 2 tablespoons grenadine

Directions

Fill cocktail shaker half full with ice. Add Applejack, lemon juice, and grenadine.

Stir with bar spoon gently to blend all ingredients. Strain into a coupe or cocktail glass that has been chilled.

Kamikaze (drink)

Ingredients

- Ice cubes
- 2 ounces vodka
- 1 ounce Blue Curacao (liqueur which tastes similar to Valencia oranges) or triple sec
- 2 tablespoons lemon juice

Directions

Fill a cocktail shaker with ice until half full. Add ingredients and shake vigorously for about 10 seconds.

Strain drink into a chilled rocks glass.

Kamikaze (shot)

Ingredients

- Ice cubes
- 1 ounce vodka
- 1 tablespoon triple sec (or you can use Blue Curacao)
- 1tablespoon fresh lemon juice

Directions

Fill shaker with ice about half way. Add all ingredients and shake hard for 10 seconds.

Strain into a chilled shot glass.

Lemon Drop

Ingredients

- Ice cubes

- 1 ½ ounces lemon flavored vodka
- 3 teaspoons triple sec (orange flavored liqueur)
- 1 ½ teaspoons simple syrup
- 3 teaspoons fresh lemon juice
- Sugar

Directions

Fill a shaker half full of ice. Add all ingredients *except* sugar. Shake well for 10 seconds.

Strain drink into a chilled cocktail glass rimmed in sugar.

Long Island Iced Tea

Ingredients

- Ice cubes
- 1 ounce vodka
- 1 ounce gin
- 1 ounce light rum
- 1 ounce white tequila
- 3 teaspoons triple sec
- 2 tablespoons fresh lemon juice

- ½ cup Coca-Cola
- Lemon wedge

Directions

Fill shaker with ice until half full. Add vodka, gin, rum, tequila, triple sec and lemon juice. Shake vigorously for 10 seconds.

Strain drink into a highball glass filled with ice. Top off with Coca-Cola and add a lemon wedge.

Mai Tai

Ingredients

- Ice cubes
- 1 ½ ounces light rum
- 1 ½ tablespoons dark rum
- 3 teaspoons orange liqueur
- 2 tablespoons pineapple juice
- 1 1/2 teaspoons lime juice
- 1 tablespoon orange juice
- Cherries for garnish

Directions

Fill shaker half way with ice. Add all ingredients and shake very vigorously for about 10 seconds.

Strain drink into a Collins or highball glass filled with ice. Garnish with a cherry.

Margarita

Ingredients

- Ice cubes
- 2 ounces white tequila (use a high-quality tequila)
- 2 tablespoons Cointreau (triple sec)
- 1 ½ tablespoons fresh lime juice
- Coarse salt
- Lime wheels or wedges

Directions

Fill a cocktail shaker with ice until half full. Add tequila, triple sec and lime juice. Shake hard for 10 seconds.

Slide a lime wedge or wheel around the rim of a margarita or rocks glass and dip into salt.

Strain margarita into a glass and add lime wedge or wheel as garnish.

Mayan Mule

Ingredients

- Ice cubes
- 2 ounces good quality tequila
- 3 teaspoons fresh lime juice
- 2 dashes Angostura bitters
- Ginger beer
- Lime wheel

Directions

Put a few ice cubes into a Collins glass. Add lime juice first, then tequila. Add ginger beer and bitters last. Stir with a bar spoon and place a lime wheel on the glass to garnish.

Mimosa
(This drink is made in a pitcher and serves 4)

Ingredients

- 8 ounces orange juice
- 1 bottle dry champagne (750 ml)
- 2 ounces triple sec or orange liqueur
- Orange curls (rind of orange)

Directions

Rinse 4 champagne glasses and stick in the freezer for a couple of hours.

When ready to serve, pour 2 ounces of orange juice into the bottom of the champagne glasses. Add champagne and fill almost to the top but not quite.

Top each glass with a splash of triple sec and garnish with the orange curl.

Mind Eraser

Ingredients

- Ice cubes
- 2 ounces vodka
- 2 ounces coffee liqueur (Kahlua)
- 2 ounces tonic water

Directions

Fill rocks glass with ice. Add vodka, coffee liqueur, and tonic water. Stir gently and serve.

Mojito

Ingredients

- Ice cubes
- 2 ounces white rum
- 1 ½ tablespoons lime juice
- 1 ounce simple syrup
- 3 teaspoons club soda, chilled
- 9 mint leaves

Directions

In a cocktail shaker, muddle 8 of the 9 mint leaves. Add ice until it is filled half full. Add rum, lime juice, and simple syrup. Shake vigorously for 10 seconds.

Fill a Collins glass with ice and strain drink into glass. Add club soda and slowly stir with a bar spoon. Add the last mint leaf for garnish.

Monte Carlo

Ingredients

- Ice cubes
- 2 ounces rye whiskey
- 3 teaspoons Benedictine (French liqueur made with herbs)
- 2 dashes Angostura Bitters

Directions

Fill cocktail shaker half full of ice. Add all ingredients and stir gently. Strain drink into a cocktail glass.

Moscow Mule

Ingredients

- Ice cubes
- ¼ cup vodka
- 1 tablespoons fresh lime juice
- ½ cup chilled ginger beer
- Lime wedge

Directions

Fill Collins or highball glass with ice. Add vodka and lime juice. Add chilled ginger beer and stir gently with a bar spoon. Put lime wedge on top as a garnish.

Paradise

Ingredients

- Ice cubes
- 2 ounces gin
- 2 ounces apricot brandy
- 2 ounces orange juice
- Orange wedge

Directions

Fill a cocktail shaker with ice half full. Add gin, brandy, and orange juice. Shake for 10 seconds.

Strain into a chilled cocktail glass and add orange wedge for a garnish.

Pina Colada
(makes 2 servings)

Ingredients

- Ice cubes
- 4 ounces spiced rum
- 4 ounces coconut milk
- 1/3 cup frozen pineapple chunks (use fresh if you can)
- 1 splash pineapple juice

Directions

Put rum, coconut milk pineapple chunks and pineapple juice in a blender. Mix until all ingredients are combined well. Add ice and blend again.

Pour into tulip glasses.

Rob Roy

Ingredients

- Ice cubes
- 2 ounces Scotch whiskey
- 1 ounce sweet vermouth
- Dash of Angostura bitters
- Maraschino cherry

Directions

Fill cocktail shaker half full with ice. Add whiskey, vermouth and bitters. With a bar spoon, blend all ingredients. Strain into a chilled cocktail glass. Add Maraschino cherry for garnish.

Ruby

Ingredients

- Ice cubes
- 1 ½ ounces citrus flavored vodka
- 3 teaspoons triple sec

- 3 ounces grapefruit juice blend (Ocean Spray Ruby Red Grapefruit juice)
- 2 teaspoons crème de cassis (liqueur made from black currants)
- Coarse brown sugar
- Candied orange slice (optional)

Directions

Fill a cocktail shaker with ice until half full. Add vodka, triple sec, grapefruit juice. Shake well for about 20 seconds.

Wet rim of a cocktail glass and dip into brown sugar. Strain drink into glass. Slowly add the crème de cassis and garnish the drink with a candied orange slice.

Screwdriver

Ingredients

- Ice cubes
- 1 ½ ounces vodka (use high-quality vodka)
- 6 ounces of fresh orange juice without pulp

Directions

Fill a cocktail shaker with ice half way. Add orange juice and vodka. Shake well and strain into a highball glass filled with ice.

Sea Breeze

Ingredients

- Ice cubes
- 2 ounces vodka
- 4 ounces cranberry juice
- 2 tablespoons grapefruit juice
- Frozen lime wedge

Directions

Fill a shaker half full of ice. Add vodka and both kinds of juice. Shake well for about 10 seconds. Fill highball or Collins glass with ice and strain drink into glass. Add frozen lime wedge for a garnish.

Sex on the Beach

Ingredients

- Ice cubes
- 1 ½ ounces vodka
- 1 ½ ounces peach schnapps
- 3 ounces cranberry juice
- 3 ounces orange juice
- Splash of lemon juice
- Lemon wheel
- Cherry

Directions

Fill a cocktail shaker with ice until half full. Add vodka, peach schnapps, and lemon juice. Shake vigorously for 10 seconds.

Strain drink into a chilled highball glass filled with ice. Add cranberry juice and orange juice. Garnish with lemon wheel and a cherry.

Singapore Sling

Ingredients

- Ice cubes
- 1 ½ ounces gin
- 3 teaspoons cherry liqueur
- 1 ½ teaspoons Cointreau (triple sec)
- 1 ½ teaspoons Benedictine
- 4 ounces pineapple juice
- 3 teaspoons lime juice
- 2 teaspoons grenadine
- 1 dash Angostura Bitters
- Slice of pineapple
- Cherry

Directions

Fill a cocktail shaker with ice until half full. Add all ingredients except the pineapple slice and the cherry.
Shake vigorously for at least 10 seconds.

Strain into a Collins glass filled with ice. Add pineapple slice and cherry for a garnish.

Spiced Pear Bellini

Ingredients

- Ice cubes
- 1 ½ ounces pear nectar (you can find this in most grocery stores)
- 1 teaspoon pear brandy
- 3 ounces champagne
- Dash nutmeg or cinnamon
- Very thin pear slice

Directions

Fill a cocktail shaker with a little ice. Add the pear nectar and the pear brandy. Stir with a bar spoon until combined.

Add champagne and stir gently for about 10 seconds. Strain into a chilled champagne glass and sprinkle with a dash of nutmeg or cinnamon and add pear slice.

Surfer on Acid

Ingredients

- Ice cubes
- 1 ounce Jagemeister (German bitter liqueur)
- 1 ounce rum
- 1 ounce pineapple juice

Directions

Fill a cocktail shaker with ice until half full. Add Jagermeister, rum and pineapple juice. Shake vigorously for 10 seconds.

Strain into a chilled cocktail glass.

Tequila Mockingbird

Ingredients

- Ice cubes

- 2 ounces tequila
- 1 ½ tablespoons crème de menthe
- 2 tablespoons fresh lime juice
- Lime wedge

Directions

Fill a cocktail shaker with ice until half full. Add tequila, crème de menthe, and lime juice. Shake vigorously for 10 seconds.

Strain into a chilled cocktail glass and add lime wedge as a garnish.

Tequila Sunrise

Ingredients

- Ice cubes
- 1 ½ ounces tequila
- ¾ cup fresh orange juice
- 3 teaspoons grenadine
- Orange slice
- Cherry

Directions

Fill a cocktail shaker with ice until half full. Add tequila and orange juice. Shake for 10 seconds.

Strain into a Collins glass filled with ice. Slowly pour in the grenadine. After grenadine settles, add the orange slice and cherry for a garnish.

Texas Two-Step

Ingredients

- Ice cubes
- 2 ounces tequila
- 2 ounces rum
- 1 ½ teaspoons blue Curacao
- 1 ½ teaspoons Cointreau (triple sec)
- Splash of lime juice
- Dash of sour mix
- Orange twist

Directions

Fill a cocktail shaker with ice until half full. Add everything except the orange twist and shake vigorously for 10 to 15 seconds.

Strain into a chilled cocktail glass and add the orange twist for a garnish.

Tom Collins

Ingredients

- Ice cubes
- 2 ounces gin
- 1 ½ tablespoons lemon juice
- 3 teaspoons simple syrup
- 2 ounces club soda
- Lemon wedge

Directions

Fill cocktail shaker half full of ice. Add gin, lemon juice, and simple syrup. Shake well for 10 seconds until very cold.

Strain into a chilled Collins glass filled with ice. Add club soda and lemon wedge as a garnish.

Transfusion

Ingredients

- Ice cubes
- 2 ounces vodka
- 2 ounces ginger ale
- 2 ounces concord grape juice
- Lime wedge

Directions

Fill a highball glass with ice. Add vodka, ginger ale and grape juice. Stir gently with a bar spoon and top off with a squeeze of the lime wedge. Add wedge and serve.

Whiskey Sour

Ingredients

- Ice cubes
- 1 ½ ounces of your favorite whiskey
- 4 ounces sour mix
- Maraschino cherry

Directions

Fill a cocktail shaker with ice until half full. Add whiskey and sour mix. Shake for 10 seconds.

Strain into a Collins or highball glass filled with ice. Add cherry.

White Russian

Ingredients

- Ice cubes
- 2 ounces vodka
- 2 tablespoons coffee liqueur
- 3 tablespoons heavy cream

Directions

Fill a rocks glass or old fashioned glass with ice. Add vodka and coffee liqueur. Stir with a bar spoon until combined. Add cream.

Zombie

Ingredients

- Ice cubes
- 1 ounce light rum
- 1 ounce dark rum
- 1 ounce apricot liqueur
- 2 ounces orange juice
- Dash lime bitters
- 1 shot of Bacardi 151 rum

Directions

Fill a cocktail shaker with ice half way. Add rum, apricot liqueur, orange juice and bitters. Shake vigorously for 10 long seconds.

Strain into a Collins glass filled with ice. Top off with a shot of Bacardi 151.

CHAPTER 7

BAR MEASUREMENTS

Measurements are probably one of the most important aspects of bartending and one of the most confusing because there is not an absolute standard.

These charts may help.

Basic Bar Measurements

Term	US Measurement	Metric Measurement
1 part	Any equal part	Any equal part
Dash	1/32 fluid ounce	.9 ml
Splash	1/12 fluid ounce	2-3 ml
1 teaspoon (tsp)	1/6 fluid ounce	4.93ml

1 tablespoon (tbsp.)	½ fluid ounce	14.79 ml
1 count	½ fluid ounce	14.79ml
1pony	1 fluid ounce	29.57 ml
1 measure	1 fluid ounce	26.5 ml
1 jigger	1 ½ fluid ounces	44.36 ml
1 shot	1 ½ fluid ounces	44.36 ml
1 miniature (nip)	2 fluid ounces	59.2 ml
1 snit	3 fluid ounces	88.72 ml
1 wineglass	4 fluid ounces	118.29 ml
1 split	6 fluid ounces	177.44 ml
1 cup	8 fluid ounces	236.58 ml
1 tenth	12.8 fluid ounces	378.88 ml
1 Mickey	13 fluid ounces	384 ml
1 pint	16 fluid ounces	473.17 ml
1 quart	32 fluid ounces	946.35 ml
1 fifth	25.6 fluid ounces (½ gallon)	757.08 ml
1 gallon	128 fluid ounces	3785.41 ml

Ounces	Count
1/2 fluid ounce	1 count
¾ fluid ounce	2 counts
1 ¼ fluid ounces	3 counts
1 ¾ fluid ounces	4 counts
2 fluid ounces	5 counts
2 ½ fluid ounces	6 counts

Bottle Sizes

Bottle Size	Amount
½ Standard Bottle	12.68 fluid ounces /375 ml
Standard Bottle	25.36 fluid ounces/ 750 ml
Magnum	50.72 fluid ounces/ 1.5 liters
Double Magnum	101.44 fluid ounces / 3 liters
Jeroboam	101.44 fluid ounces / 3 liters
Rehoboam	152.06 fluid ounces/ 1.19 fluid gallons /4.5 liters

Bender Barware

www.ingramcontent.com/pod-product-compliance
Lightning Source LLC
Chambersburg PA
CBHW070157290526
45789CB00002B/806